MONSTERS
COLOR BY NUMBERS

Isobel Lundie

HIDDEN INSIDE THIS BOOK THERE ARE:

3 mutant fish

5 dead fish

12 bones

16 flies

3 spiders

12 leaves

1 splat

2 dirty forks

2 smelly socks

2 frilly underpants

CAN YOU FIND THEM?

2

MONSTERS
COLOR BY NUMBERS

Inside this book you will find a collection of silly monsters. Use the color chart at the beginning of the book to help you choose your pencil.

When you've finished coloring, try helping the monsters on the sides of the pages to answer the monster questions.

GOOD LUCK

MEET THE MONSTERS...

Look at at all these very silly monsters. Can you find them inside the book?

GHOUL WITH THE PEARL EARRING

PAUL

SQUIGGILY-DIGGILY

DODGE

KING HORRID

PETE

MATCHO

4

FLUMP

FREAK-DA KHALO

DINA

SMUG DOUG

BERNARD

ROCTOPUS

PI

ITCHY

BEEFY

5

MONSTER SPACE

What color is the light coming from the rocket?
. . . .

What color is the monster holding the rocket?
. . . .

What color is the moon?
. . . .

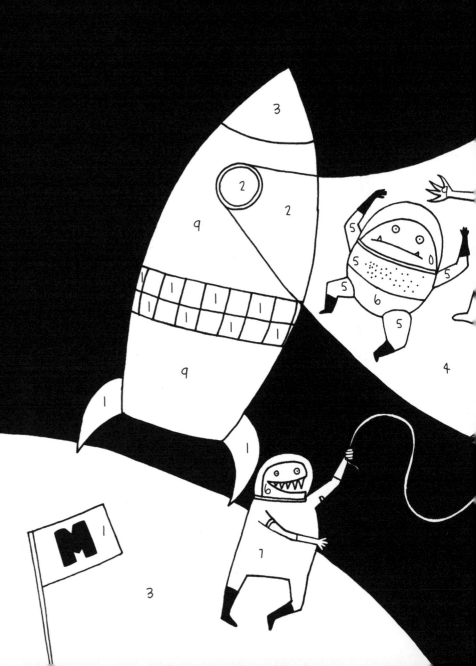

MONSTER MARATHON

What color clothes is the winning monster wearing?
....

Are there any orange monsters running the race?
....

What color is the running track?
....

14

MONSTER MUSEUM

Can you name any of these famous monster portraits?
. . . .

What color is the ghoul with the pearl earring?
. . . .

What color is the wall of the museum?
. . . .

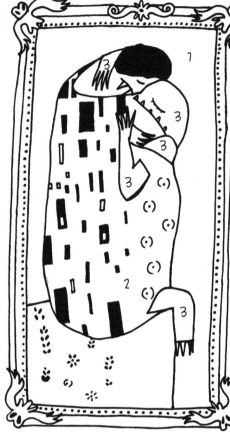

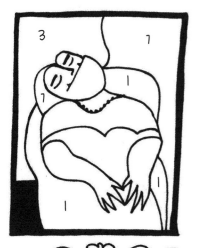

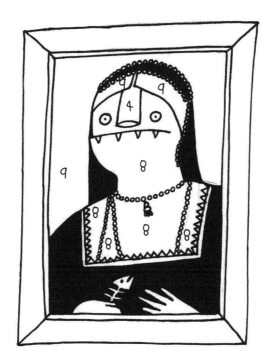

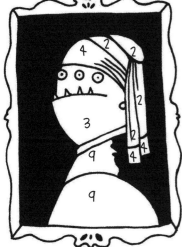

2

MONSTER MUSEUM

How many portraits have green monsters in them?
. . . .

What color is freak-da khalo?
. . . .

What color are the picture frames?
. . . .

17

MONSTER FUNFAIR

What color is the monster who is pretending to be a horse?
......

Are there any pink monsters riding the carousel?
......

What color are the horses?
......

MONSTER ISLAND

How many monsters are sitting on the monster island?
......

Is the monster island orange with blue stripes?
....

What color is the water?
......

MONSTER WASHING

What color is the fluffy monster?
......

How many monsters are hanging from the washing line?
....

How many smelly socks are there?
......

26

CAN YOU MAKE THESE SHAPES INTO SILLY MONSTERS?

What color clothes is the winning monster wearing?
BLUE

Are there any orange monsters running the race?
No

What color is the running track?
Red

How many gray monsters are running the marathon?
One

What color is the slowest monster?
Green

What color is the ribbon?
Yellow

Can you name any of these famous monster portraits?
....

What color is the ghoul with the pearl earring?
Gray

What color is the wall of the museum?
Yellow

How many portraits have green monsters in them?
Four

What color is freak-da khalo?
Pink

What color are the picture frames?
White

What color is the two-headed dog?
Green

How many monsters have got their eyes closed?
Two

Are there any brown monsters?
No

What color is the blue monster's tongue?
Pink

How many pink monsters are there?
Two

What color is the pilot's scarf?
Purple

32

33